A TUNE A DAY

FOR CLASSICAL GUITAR.

BY C. PAUL HERFURTH
AND STANLEY GEORGE URWIN.

Book One.

BRET	
DOGS	
EYE	
ORTON	1|01
STAN	
THORN	
WERR	
WHIT	
WOOD	
YAXL	
PEMOB	
SMOP	

Exclusive Distributors:
Music Sales Limited
8/9 Frith Street, London W1V 5TZ, England.
Music Sales Pty Limited
120 Rothschild Avenue, Rosebery, NSW 2018, Australia.

Order No. BM10124
ISBN 0.7119.1560.1

BOSTON MUSIC COMPANY.